Through the Ash

Jazzarae Krebs

BookLeaf Publishing

Presentation by *BookLeaf Publishing*

Web: www.bookleafpub.com

E-mail: info@bookleafpub.com

ISBN: 9789357440332

First edition 2023

*To all those who helped shape me to the woman
I am today. Both negative and positive, I
wouldn't be who I am without you.*

Damage

It must have been an
Internal wound
Because God damn did I bleed
And it pooled into
My eyes   so I couldn't see
My ears   so I couldn't hear
My lungs   so I couldn't breathe
I took your sadness as my own
I seen you
I heard you
I breathed you
That's the trouble with wounds like these
You can feel the pain
But can't see the damage
And with wounds like these
They kill you
Always in the end
They suck the life out of you
And they kill you.

Black Hole

He compared me to the sun
A swirling mass of
Heat, pressure, and metamorphosis
Constantly pulling anything in its orbit
slowly closer to its burning core
I finally wonder if the sun
isn't terribly alone
So beautiful, so majestic
So dangerous
He compared me to the sun as a gift
But I felt the curse there
How horrible it must be to suck worlds
In around you as you devour
the company you desperately seek
Growing bigger, stronger, hotter as
You consume their spark
Does she cry out in pain and sorrow
Does she finally wish to explode
Into the dark

Never Enough

They watched in horror
in fascination
As I picked up the knife
capturing everyone's attention
Staring at his beautiful eyes
They gasped
Is I slipped the tip of the sharpest blade
into my chest
Who would have guessed what would come next
Cracking ribs, severing tendons, destroying
myself to let myself free
As I cut my chest open,
As I took my heart out,
As I soaked myself in blood
Each pump
Pushing
Gushing
Spilling
Dripping down my hands and soaking my arms
Rushing out onto the wooden floor
The definition of self-harm
I knew the truth
The only truth
He wanted what they all wanted
All of me

And I had spent so long trying to please
That I wrapped myself in pretty silk ribbons
And smiled and shivered in ecstasy
and when he wanted more
I poured, and I poured and
I poured
and when I heard it wasn't enough
I grabbed my heart
and with my own bare hands
I wrung her dry
I never spoke a word of it,
you never heard me cry
and when it was finished
and I had given all I could
I looked up into those eyes
Begging without words
That what I did was good
Begging without words
That it was enough
and that I was good.

Sin

I've lost it
all I've ever dreamed
everything I want
it's all in my imagination
it was all just a taunt
but I held it in my hand
and I promised myself I wouldn't let it go
and now I've ruined everything
I've gotten nothing left to show
but a sickness in my heart
and despise in my soul
I'm such a stupid selfish girl
who still hasn't learned to just say no
I would suffocate my dreams and be dragged
along again
I'm an inconsiderate lover full to the brim with
all this sin
You could have been my salvation, my heart, my
life, my love
but I let you down as well
and it gives my heart a shove
why can't I be strong like you
love like you
be like you
be with you

because I am weak
and cannot find the courage in my soul
to hurt the one that is as weak as me,
I'm sure it's a feeling that you know
and I can give you no excuses
for there is not much I can say
my dream is to be like you
so strong and sure someday
I take my heart in my hand
and it tear it into to shreds
for now inside by body things have stopped,
and all I feel is dread,,
for the future I have accepted
and life I will force myself to live
but remember there is nothing
you could ask of me,
that I wouldn't try to give
and I wish we had more time together
but I guess that wouldn't be the best
I'm sorry that I hurt you so,
I didn't want to be like the rest
I wanted to make you happy
and I wanted to make you laugh
but there is this weight that is tied to my chest
and I just don't know what to do with that
you're an amazing self-righteous person
and I hope to see you again
and no matter how much you hate me,
you'll always be my friend.

Cancer

It poured out
like a cork popped lose
I scrambled to close it
tried to squeeze my fingers
into the overflowing hole
But it was already in motion
I was going to pay the toll

I collapsed to the ground
As it poured out on to the hot asphalt
As I watched all I had ever built
All I had ever hoped for
Evaporate into thin air
Not even a chance to scrap it back up
It disappeared without a care

While I watched it disappearing
I finally understood what it meant
to be immeasurable
I watched it consume me
Grief, Anger, Pain
Visions of me screaming, yelling,
It took everything to keep me sane

As everything I ever built, bleed for,
Worked to the bone for,
drained away
It was gone. Gone in one second
How could one word create so much doubt
Broken and bleeding, they said pick yourself
back up
you have just moments to figure it out.

Sibling rivalry

So let me tell you what is on my mind
Every time he calls
I don't know what to say
because he is filled with love
and all of these good memories
I listen to the tales of them together
Then I go back to struggling
just to get through my day
He will never understand
The pain and the anger
The disappoint that   it eats me
The sadness   that it engulfs
me
I think all the time like;
How
Could
You
Have
Ever
Died
Hell, he will never know what's on my mind
How some days I hate you with a rage so deep
And others I miss you with an
Unquenchable sadness that never ceases to seep
I always grasped for the love

That he was handed so easily
Tring to be the strong one
But breaking down to my knees
And it all comes down to the
Hurt and the pain
The sadness and the shame
The overwhelming disrespect
That I was forced to just deflect
That fact that he was her boy
and I was just another girl
We lived in the same household
but grew up in two different worlds
He would be ashamed if he knew what was on
my mind
I am ashamed that it's there after all this time
Oh, but now he has heard what is on my mind
Damn, he will hate me too for what is on my
mind
I wish I could keep it all inside
But the truth is,
It was always on my mind.

Masterpiece

Its breath taking to think
All her life her words had
Created pictures of pain and sorrow
But she wanted to create mountains
Majestic mountains built tall and strong
And rivers flowing deep and wide
And it would be him, who gave it to her
Him who handed it over in stride
One day she woke up and was free
All to the strength he had given so easily
Her heart burst with happiness
Her blood flowed with life
And she'd never been so grateful
To be called this man's wife
She felt beautiful and light as air
She could finally live her life without a care
All because he took the sorrow
He swallowed up the pain
He gave her a new life
And gave her a new name

Over the Edge

Leap
I whisper
As I watch you at the edge
Leap
I whisper
As I watch you catch your breath
Leap
I whisper
I know the ledge is cloud in mist
Leap
I whisper
This is the chance I don't want to miss
I close my eyes tight
I can feel it in the air
then I feel your lips on mine
Your hands wrapped in my hair
Ecstasy and bliss
I wrap my arms around your neck
I stare out at the ledge again
As a darkness swirls inside
He never took that leap of faith
He never held his breath
He never dove all the way in
But he wants to give me what is left
Leap

I whisper
As I hold my hand to my heart Inside my chest
Leap
I whisper
As I turn away from you and
tumble of the cliff

Ash

I look up and it quickens
Our eyes meet
My heart beats
And I catch on fire
Sometimes it does very much indeed
Feel just that way
My skin ignites under your fingertips,
My mind ignites under your words,
I'd give anything for an hour in front of you,
I'd give anything for an hour to burn
Does it feel like peace? Does it feel like war?
It feels like I will completely explode away
Leaving behind nothing but my core
I hope when you see the liquid molten center
The harden spots where nothing has moved
the spots that spit out lava and grief
you can still feel the softness underneath
I hope you love it like God loves hurricanes
Raw power, immeasurable beauty,
And pain.
Stand inside the storm with me,
We can jump into the wind
We can catch the whole world on fire
And make love to our grief

Rosemary

It just goes beyond reason
This girl was just starting her first season
But watch her she is so amazing
Drop down and worship at her angle

She stops the birds in mid flight
The very earth holds its breath at night
Don't hesitate, don't think, just jump in
You will do so much more than just live

Oh, rosemary life can be hard
It's not fair and it can break apart your heart
But its beauty is truly indescribable
And its miracles are undeniable

Rosemary, precious little sweetheart
I am so sorry you've had to taste the dark
It'll change who you are meant to be
And you'll transcend through history
Don't ever look back behind you
Those things are no longer meant for you
Keep your head up and forward
I'll be you shield and armor

You change everyone around you
Anyone who has ever met you
Your soul speaks more for you
You've got the heart of a warrior

Savior

Lost in a world of books,
How can I live so far from reality?
Trapped, wrapped,
I am so completely lost.
Who can come and take me from this fantasy?
Who can rip my brain so incased,
So covered and converted,
From its most cherished
Place?
Can you destroy all my happiness
And show me the light?
Gag me bound me drown me
And end all the fights
Suffocate the imagination
And tear apart the dreams
Smash crush rip
And disintegrate me
Burn the beautiful pages
And pull out my eyes
I Criss cross my heart
I will never Read again
Of course I'm feeding you lies
If you take away reading
You will destroy my soul
Pound, stab, choke

There would be none of me to behold
To take away reading
Would be to take a way a life
To cage, beat, and hypnotize
Do you really think that's right

Don't look back

Help me lose my self
And escape what can no longer
Be mine
This cannot be home,
I must leave this life behind
I must open my soul
And let it finally breathe
This is all about becoming
A bigger better me
You can do this on your own
Your stronger than you think
Just immerse yourself in your life
And fulfill your wildest dreams
Youve been the best thing in my life,
And created so much joy
But if I stay here for long
I'll turn into a toy
A perfectionist doll
Whose life has left her eyes
I'll sit and do nothing
Your love will turn into despise
I must fulfill my calling
And I must do it alone
But The strongest love to me,
you have always shown

I could never repay you
And will be indebt forever
But forgive me my love
There are somethings we cannot
Do together
They say to find true love
You must let things go
Will you keep me here
trapped by saying no?
There is heart break in my chest
And tears choking my lungs
I can no longer breathe
But this still isn't done
Kiss me goodbye and
Dry the tears that have fallen
I'm finally leaving,
it's time to fulfill
My life's true calling

Be Mine

Spark ignite consume
the connection formed between
glances into the soul
through eyes wide, hearts willing
and the world and all we know
the soul seeps warmth into the body
excited to show, to spend, to learn
to share what creates one, with another
and all the love that we have yearned
words words words, paint pictures of
fantasies not yet filled, but aching
to be achieved.
breaking over imaginary boundaries,
crashing into the imagination,
and waiting to be relieved,
a few moments,
a trifle little amount of time,
to search the deepness in your eyes,
and see if you wanted to be mine
a glimpse of something tempting,
in those vivid beautiful eyes
a hope for newer experiences,
I was exceptionally surprised

Lust

It sucks every other thought away,
It begins to suffocate my senses,
and at the same time brighten my day.
If I feel with my heart,
I will choke up and cry,
From this life taking energy,
And I'll tell you just why.
It can Plunge me into the coldest of cold
To where it is the only source of heat,
There's no alternative to behold.
It can suck me down into the
Bottom of the sea,
Where I look up through the light,
And where the energy is
Is where I want to be,
It wraps me tight in its gripping arms,
there is no other choice to be had
If I could give it up I would
But it's not a passing fad
Its lifts me up and soars to the top of the clouds,
And without this energy I could not survive,
I just I wouldn't know how
As I look now to the source of this intoxicating
energy,
I find its really just depleting

It comes from the ache inside
From a love that was always leaving

Death

24

It smells like sick
The unrelenting attack on
unsuspecting flesh
It seeps through your mask
It floods your soul
Never in my life will I forget
The smell
Saturating everything
Drowning everything
Sweet and deadly
It smells like sick

Self reflection

I wasn't worth a house
I know
But I was worth a heart
And I wasn't worth the sadness
I know
But I was worth a start
I wasn't worth it at all to you
I know
But
I found all these things I was worthy of
When you found me
And when you left me
And when you drag me through the months
I was worth a green eyed gypsy
You know
One whose hands were strong and his
Anger slow
I was worth a million sunrises
You know
And I was worth so much more

Chloe

I just wanted her to love me
And she wouldn't
Or she couldn't
So, I travelled the world
And all the faces
To search for her
To try to fill her place
And I met them
I seen what I seen
And felt what I felt
And it shot me back
To then and there
And when and how
And all the bullshit I allowed
I told myself I would never
Be that kid again
And here I am
Feeling just like I did
Watching her pretend
Trying so hard to figure out
How to help
To step back or step up
To sit by or stand down
Because who am I to do
Anything at all

I could never even help myself
I've always felt so small

Keep going

Push it down
There is far too much to do
Push it down
You can handle this
You've had more you've had to do
So when your heart breaks and you can hardly
breathe
Push it down babe
You've got places to go
People to be

Live

And they said everything happens for a reason
But that breaks me even more
For who could wish for cancer,
A girl not even four
So, I watch, I scream, I cry,
I hide it all inside
Because what can you do
Your only choices are to fight
Fight fight fight
Give it all away
Because that's all we have
Don't count your days
Don't count your breaths
Live, live, live,
until there is nothing left
You are so very cursed
You are so very blessed
So live, breath, explore,
Don't think about the rest
Because one day the chance is gone
And you've stayed in one place for far too long
Leave the luggage, leave the friends,
leave it now and don't look back again

Daydream

I could feel the blush
Spread all the way to my toes.
The feeling that shoots down inside you,
If you know, then you know
The way the colors in the air suspended
And formed a halo around his face
The moment took away my breath
And it's a moment I wouldn't waste
He slowly placed his hands on either side of my
head
 his fingers slowly caressing my cheeks
Is my heart still beating?
Am I alive or am I dead,
His thumb slides across my lip,
And my heart begins to dip,
The moan escapes my mouth
And suddenly gasp out loud.

Stalking

I used to think the devil loved me
I used to imagine he placed kisses on my lips
I used to think the devil loved me
I fell for all his tricks
I used to think the devil loved me
As his hands ran through my wings
I used to think the devil loved me
Especially when he'd sing
I used to think the devil loved me
Before he sewed tight my lips
I used to think the devil loved me
Until he sawed my wings off at the tip
I used to think the devil loved me
Until his words began to sting
I used to think the devil loved
What a stupid stupid thing

www.ingramcontent.com/pod-product-compliance
Lightning Source LLC
Chambersburg PA
CBHW070724160726
48003CB00006BA/2370